A Pipe Hitter's Guide to

Access Denial

"You Shall Not Pass"

by

Nicholas Orr

with

Jeff Kirkham

A Pipe Hitter's Guide to Access Denial

"You Shall Not Pass"

by

Nicholas Orr
with Jeff Kirkham
Copyright 2023
All Rights Reserved

Cover Design: Zachary Markel

You Shall Not Pass 2

Acknowledgments

For this third installment in the Pipe Hitters series, I tapped two of my most valuable resources; Jeff Kirkham and Paul Markel.

Jeff Kirkham is a true renaissance man. He has been both a killer and a healer. As a Green Beret, Mr. Kirkham spent decades overseas dealing out hate and discontent. However, Jeff also invented the RATS; a rapid tourniquet that has been used to save countless lives during the last ten years. Not content to administer battlefield medicine, he went to school and became a Registered Nurse. Jeff is a prolific author and also owns and operates www.ReadyMan.com.

Paul Markel became a United States Marine in 1987 and is a combat decorated veteran. Mr. Markel has been a state-certified Police Officer as well as an Executive Protection Agent. During the recent unpleasantness, Markel worked as a Military Contractor and trained thousands of troops as a Small Arms & Tactics Instructor.

Paul founded www.StudentoftheGun.com in 2010 as a media production entity. He also has over 30 books published and a thousand plus articles to his name.

I am indebted to both of these men for their contribution. It is highly suggested that you seek out their written works and study them.

Also, I must once more acknowledge and thank Zachary Markel for his patience and effort in working with me on the cover design. I could not have done it without him.

P.S. As we would suggest with any instructional or educational text, please keep a pencil and a highlighter close at hand while reading. We absolutely encourage note taking on the pages within.

Contents

Introduction

In the United States of America, in the 21st Century, the concept of access denial or home fortification might seem to most people to be paranoid or an over-reaction. There are, however, some places where this has been commonplace for decades.

Having grown up in Detroit, Michigan in the 1970's and 80's, I witnessed home fortification and business fortification. I grew up believing that every bank in the world had bullet-proof glass separating the customer from the teller. Ditto for every gas station and convenience store. It was not until I was in my late teens, when my family moved to another state, into a rural community, that I realized all banks and gas stations did not have bullet barriers and slots used to shove your money to the teller/cashier. I came to learn that most of America was a relatively safe place to live, the exceptions were the big cities; Detroit, New York, Chicago, New Orleans, etc.

If you were to travel to an area where the homes had bars on the windows and doors, where the businesses had roll-down steel doors to protect them after closing, you would rightly associate that area with a high crime rate. For travelers, such scenes are a big clue that you are in a crime-infested area and you do not want to linger there. Those who live in such urban cesspools come to view such scenes as commonplace. They have been brainwashed into believing that barricading your home or business against criminal vermin is just part of "life in the big city".

The majority of those living in the United States enjoy a type of safety that is completely foreign to citizens of many countries in the world. City-dwellers in Brazil, Mexico, France, Italy, India, etc. live in constant fear of robbery, burglary, and muggings. Their homes are fortified behind steel fences and gates, decorated with barbed wire. Cinder block and brick walls often have broken glass bottles placed neck down in concrete on top of them to discourage burglars from scaling them.

In many third world countries, homes are built as compounds or mini-fortresses surrounded by hardened dirt, stone, and brick walls with huge steel gates chained together to prevent unauthorized access. This is naturally a carry over from centuries of rampaging hordes and bands of roaming thieves.

Okay, so what does this have to do with the United States of America in the early stages of the 21st Century? Well, unless you have been living under a rock, you will realize that, whether by malevolence, corruption, or complete incompetence, events have been put into motion to create national and worldwide instability in the form of food and energy shortages. The international supply chain has been damaged perhaps to the point where it will break. Corrupt leaders carp on about "social justice" and "saving the environment" while ignoring border security, energy/fuel and food production. The national government of the United States is spending money like there is no tomorrow, all the while racking up TRILLIONS in debt.

As nations see their energy prices rising, their food production dwindling, and their debt increasing, the tendency to wage war as a solution magnifies. This has always been the case throughout world history. Adolf Hitler used the German economic depression to drive his country to war. Most historians also agree that President Franklin D. Roosevelt saw the United States entry into WWII as the solution to ending the Great Depression. While wars might drive the engine of production in a nation, they also extract a heavy price in blood. Wars also lead to famine and disease.

During the year 2020, the people of the United States were whipped up into a panic, deliberately. We witnessed shortages in every category almost immediately. While this situation abated after a few months of panic buying, we need to ask ourselves if anything has changed? What will the reaction of Americans be if/when Europe goes to war with Russia. What happens if/when China invades Taiwan? If a nuclear weapon detonated anywhere on the planet, how quickly would every grocery store be cleared out by panicked citizens?

How will people react when faced with the reality that food production worldwide dropped in 2022 and will continue to drop due to skyrocketing fuel and fertilizer costs? What happens to food production when farmers in the Netherlands (the world's 2nd largest exporter of food) have been punished to the point where crop production is cut in half or even cut by seventy-five percent by 2024?

Farmers in the United States fought a war on two fronts between skyrocketing fuel and fertilizer costs and a seasonal drought. We have not even discussed farmland that was made idle by US Government overreach as well as the evil hand of billionaires purchasing farmland and then letting it sit unused.

Nothing above is conspiracy and it is all verifiable from numerous sources. You simply need to extricate your cranium from your rectum and pay attention to the world around you.

Rising costs and shortages inevitably lead to theft or outright robbery. There are those who, rather than prepare themselves, see stealing your food, fuel, medicine, etc. as their solution. How do you stop them? How do you make your home and your community a hard target? That, my dear reader, is the purpose behind this book.

-Nicholas Orr, Somewhere in the United States, November 2022

Chapter 1

Fortifying your Neighborhood and Community

by Paul Markel

For decades I have listened to gun culture chest-thumpers say things like; "They better not come to my house." or some similar bravado. While such statements might be intended to make the speaker seem like a cool guy or a hardass, harsh reality has something in store for them.

Waiting for trouble to arrive at our front doorstep before we address it is the worst possible plan of action. There is a big difference between locking your doors against the unexpected / unanticipated burglar and dealing with gangs of roaming looters and thieves. Regarding such threats, the best plan of action is to keep the fight as far away from your homes; wives, children, grandchildren, as possible. Fighting on your porch or in your living room should be your last, desperate resort.

Civil unrest can break out at a moment's notice. This is particularly true in large urban environments. When the rioting begins, you will not have weeks or days even to prepare. Are you planning to drive to the local home improvement store during the riots? That's like planning to run out a purchase a gun after the civil unrest has begun. When the crisis hits, you are going to have to make due with whatever you already have on hand.

At some point you are going to have to limit and restrict access to your community and neighborhood. The larger the city in which you reside, the more difficult this will be to accomplish. Conversely, the more rural your community and remote, the easier it will be to control access. If you are living in a metropolitan area with hundreds of thousands or even millions of people, your life will be interesting indeed. Remember the fragile food supply chain? Add to the food problem, the organized drug gangs in your city whose numbers are likely in the hundreds, if not thousands.

Paul Markel (center) supervises troop training during GWOT.

Vehicles as Barriers

The fastest way to block off a street (the entrance to a neighborhood) is to pull a vehicle or vehicles across the roadway. The advantage to this method is that it can be done quickly with essentially no physical labor. The downside is that these vehicles become "sacrificial lambs" as they will be subject to being rammed by looter vehicles or shot up by armed thugs.

Keep in mind, thieves and looters will be driving stolen vehicles for which they care nothing about. If they smash up the stolen car they happen to be driving, they will just steal another one.

If you are relying on your pickup truck to transport supplies for your family, you don't want to sacrifice it to a riot demolition derby or allow it to become a bullet sponge for thugs armed with all the guns they stole from a pawn shop. If you have old, junk vehicles that can be put in place, use them. Don't sacrifice useful, utility vehicles.

Large, heavy, old vehicles are the best candidates for hasty roadblocks.

In rural communities, farm wagons and such wheeled vehicles can be used. Your John Deere combine with a corn head might look menacing, however, such things are far too valuable to be used as target practice for looters and thugs. Instead you might drag out an old manure spreader or hay wagon to quickly block a road. If the spreader is full, be sure to check the wind first.

(Skill Level: Low/Easy)

Road Spikes

Spike Board: An easy to make and easy to deploy road spike barrier can be made by taking a standard 2x6 piece of lumber and driving 60 penny (6 inch) or 70 penny (7 inch) carpentry nails through the board and staggering them. The average board is 8 feet long.

Drill a hole on each end of the board and loop a rope through each hole so that it can be pulled into place or pulled out of the way by friendly forces, quickly. The rope should be 10 to 12 feet on each end. Depending on the width of the road, you may choose to use one, two, or three of these Spike Boards. Standard lane width in the United States is 12 feet.

(Skill Level: Beginner)

Spike boards are made from common lumber.

Common and framing nails in 4, 6, and 8 inch lengths can be found in hardware stores.

Remember to get some rope to be used as drag handles for the spike board and jack rock chain.

Caltrops / Jack Rocks: Using the previously discussed 60p or 70p nails, you can produce individual road spikes that can be deployed en masse on roadways just beyond barriers or signs forbidding people to enter the road. When spread widely over a likely avenue of approach, caltrops have the added advantage of greatly slowing the advance of mobs of looters. The looters will not be able to run at or rush defenders, that is unless they want to impale their feet on the spikes. These will not stop them, but will definitely slow their roll.

To make individual road spikes, take 2 large nails and cut off the heads to create an angled point. Bend the nails approximately 45 degrees and weld the two nails together at the bends so that no matter how they land, one point will be up. Think of a child's toy jacks, only much larger.

Portable welding machines are affordable and readily available.

(Skill Level: Intermediate to Advanced)

There are a few online outlets that sell premade caltrops. One store sells them in ten packs for $50. You will likely need dozens or even hundreds, at $5 a piece that price tag adds up quickly. It might be a good idea to purchase some pre-made versions and then replicate more later.

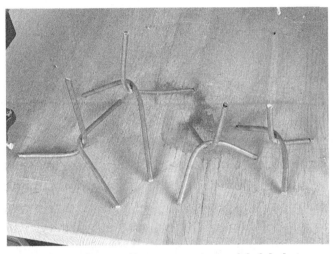

Jack rocks, caltrops, or tetsubishi date back hundreds of years.

"Jack Rocks" is the term that union men use for road spikes that they litter around the gates during labor disputes. I have collected these as souvenirs from security assignments over the years.

The Japanese call these spiky devices tetsubishi and they date back to the feudal era. One form of caltrop, that looked more like a large toy jack made of cast steel, was widely used during the American Civil War to impede cavalry troops. These were dumped on the road by the barrel full and did such horrific damage to horse hoofs that they were considered a form of barbarism or terrorism by the enemy.

As recently as 2022, caltrops were used by Ukrainian resistance forces during the Russia/Ukraine conflict. It is not surprising that history repeats itself.

Jack Rock Chain: We take the same method used to produce individual home-made caltrops and combine them with a 25 foot length of chain. Suggested link size is 5/16 inch. Starting from one end, the two caltrop pieces are inserted at 12 inch intervals. The two caltrop nails are welded together while they are inside of a chain link. As with the spike board, you will want to put some type of flexible handle on each end of the chain; rope or strap material will work. PS: at this writing, a 25 foot 5/16 inch chain from Harbor Freight was priced at $39.99.

The end result is a 25 foot long road vehicle barrier that can be rapidly deployed to stop threats or rapidly removed to allow friendly vehicles to pass. Unlike individual jack rocks that must be picked up one at a time, the chain, though heavy, is a more convenient solution. Both forms have merit depending on the situation.

(Skill Level: Intermediate to Advanced)

Sturdy chains such as these from Harbor Freight are easy to come by.

No Tool Jack Rocks: If you do not have welding equipment, you can still make some jack rocks/caltrops quickly. All you need is a box of 4-inch galvanized nails and a bag of hollow practice golf balls. You simply need to push the nails through the holes in the practice golf balls. Use four nails per ball. This will create a four-pronged caltrop that will always land with one point facing up. Plastic practice balls for golf come in white, orange, and other colors depending on where you purchase them.

If you want the caltrops to serve as a warning, leave them orange or white. If you want them to be more covert, pick up a can or two of black, dark gray or dirt brown spray paint. The next advancement of this concept would be a genuine golf ball, however to drive the nails through you will need either a hand drill or serious hammering skills. Keep an empty 5 gallon bucket handy to store your jack rocks.

(Skill Level: Beginner)

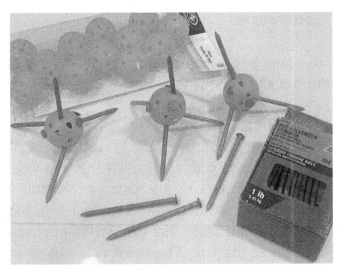

If you have no tools at all, you can still make usable jack rocks with nails and practice golf balls.

Fence Panel Caltrops   If you live in a rural area where galvanized fence panels are common, there is a jack rock / caltrop hack that requires only a section of fence panel, sturdy bolt cutters, a bench vice, and a pencil or a marker.

A fast way to measure is to use your off hand. Place the center wire between your middle and ring finger on the horizontal plane and mark the outer edge of your hand. Now turn your hand and repeat the process, only this time on the vertical plane. You now have four evenly spaced marks.

Take your bolt cutters and clip the fence wire at the marks. Repeat this process for as many jack rocks as you want to make.

The last step is to take the "t" or "plus sign" wire sections to your workbench and your vice. Clamp one end in the vice and bend it approximately 45 degrees. Now switch to the other wire and bend that one in the opposite direction of the first. The result is a caltrop or jack rock that will always land with one point facing up.

(Skill Level: Beginner)

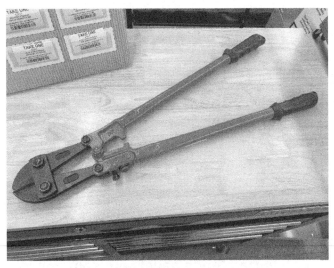

A solid set of bolt cutters is needed for the fence panel jack rocks.

Every shop should have a bench vice, they are readily available and affordable.

Galvanized fence panels are common in rural environments.

Signs and Barriers

Sawhorses: The typical sawhorse made of 2x4 lumber can be quickly assembled and used to mount traffic control signs at checkpoints. During a crisis, if you don't have a STOP sign for your roadblock you can surely find one at an intersection somewhere. A sturdy sawhorse can be dragged in and out of the road quickly.

If you are going to be putting up a checkpoint on a well-traveled road, particularly one where the speed limit is 55 mph or higher, you will need to put out signage warning traffic to SLOW DOWN and advise them that there is a CHECKPOINT ahead. These signs advising people to slow down and prepare to stop need to be far enough out to actually give drivers ample time to slow down and not crash into your barricade material or other vehicles. Remember, we want to aid the good people while we are weeding out the bad people.

Being forewarned that they are approaching a checkpoint that is likely manned by armed good guys, many bad guys will decide to turn around and go somewhere else. Or, and we need to assume this, they will attempt to circumnavigate the checkpoint in some other way.

A Deadly serious sign for serious times.

For suburban neighborhoods and cul-de-sac communities, a large sign affixed to a sawhorse that states "Looters Will Be Shot" might seem a bit dramatic. Nonetheless, the middle of a riot is not the time to be sensitive. "Looters Will Be Shot" or "Deadly Force Authorized" are warnings that cannot be misconstrued even by the most sub-moronic thug.

(Skill Level: Easy/Beginner)

This "Danger" sign gives ample warning.

Simple and to the point.

Hedgehog: A hedgehog looks like a giant caltrop or tetsubishi. During WWI and WWII hedgehogs were constructed of steel "I" beam material to impede tanks on roads and landing craft on beaches. For our purposes, we can make hedgehogs out of 4x4 lumber. You will need 4 foot pieces of 4x4, heavy duty bolts, washers and nuts and/or 90° corner braces/brackets (heavy duty) and wood screws that are at least 3 inches long.

Lay two pieces of 4x4 centered atop one another in a "+" sign configuration. Secure them together with a heavy duty bolt. Now take the third piece of 4x4 and center it on the other two, making a three-dimensional cross or "t". When it is complete you have your six-pointed wooden hedgehog. If you require larger hedgehogs just alter the length of your 4x4.

(Skill Level: Beginner)

After you have made several wooden hedgehogs you can spread them out and run barbed wire between them to create a barrier that can be quickly deployed across a road or pathway or any likely area of approach. While it is true that a hedgehog will not stop a car or truck, any person that drives over one, particularly when wrapped in barbed wire, is not going to be happy.

Hedgehogs from common lumber

55 Gallon Drums / Barrels: If you need to create barriers that will stop or slow down vehicles, 55 gallon drums are an easy solution. A 55 gallon plastic barrel filled with water will weigh around 450 pounds. If you set them up in a triangle formation touching one another, that gives you 1300 plus pounds of barrier. A long tie-down/ratchet strap can be wrapped around the barrels to secure them as a single unit.

The benefit of plastic barrels is that they can be staged easily and then topped off with water. The downside, naturally, is that if they are punctured the water will leak out rendering them useless. Water barrels can be used for cover only for a short time.

Conversely, if you can get your hands on steel 55 gallon drums and fill them with sand, each one will weigh over 800 pounds. Put the sand filled drums in a triangle formation and you have over one full ton of weight. That will slow down any standard passenger car or light truck. Steel drums filled with sand will naturally provide cover from small arms fire as well.

(Skill Level: Beginner)

Plastic water barrels are easy to stage and extremely heavy when filled.

Sandbags: Sandbags are easy to come by and not that expensive. You can purchase the industrial variety that will be white, orange or some other color. The surplus market also is a good place to find military OD green sandbags. Naturally, plain white sandbags are the least expensive. Expect to pay $30 to $40 for 100 white sandbags.

Sandbags have been used to build cover for armies for a hundred years or more. They are versatile but they are also labor intensive to fill. Filling sandbags is definitely a team project. Note: In the event of an ongoing crisis, you must remember to maintain security during the construction process. Double thick walls of sandbags should stop any conventional small arms you might be facing (.50 BMG is a different story).

When reinforcing guard posts or checkpoints with sandbags, the normal configuration will be a "U" or three-sided square with the opening facing the secure area. The sandbag wall should be built up to the sternum of the average man; think 4 to 4.5 feet tall.

(Skill Level: Beginner)

Sandbags are a must have.

Gabion / Hesco Barriers: The "Gabion" is a centuries old invention whereby a wire-cage, wooden box structure or even a large wicker basket, is strategically put in place and then filled with rocks, dirt, or sand. During GWoT, these devices were mass produced and shipped overseas under the name "HESCO".

The Hesco barrier or the Hesco bastion was used to rapidly construct walls around bases. Hesco barriers were relatively lightweight wire cages with liners that would hold in sand. Modern Hesco barriers vary in size, but, when filled with hard packed sand they weigh hundreds or thousands of pounds. Unlike sandbags which are labor intensive and time consuming to fill, a Hesco barrier can be set up by a few men and filled with a front loader (farm or commercial) in a relatively short amount of time.

Gabion cages are readily available from many landscaping or home improvement stores. You can order them online if you like. The modern gabion cages do not have liners so they need to be filled with rocks. If you have more sand available to you than rocks, you will need to secure some type of liner for your gabion cages. However, if you live in a rocky area, you are all set.

Both the Hesco and gabion will perform double duty as vehicle barriers and effective cover from small arms fire. A hard packed, rock filled gabion that is 3 feet thick will stop a .50 BMG (at least the first couple of shots, a full belt will destroy your gabion. Hopefully, that won't be an issue)

The biggest caution to be offered regarding the Hesco / Gabion barrier is to carefully and deliberately choose the location. Once erected, they will weigh thousands of pounds. These are not something you are going to want to be moving around.

Large gabion or Hesco barriers can be placed across roads to completely block traffic or, more practically, they are placed in a staggered pattern to force vehicles to slow down to a crawl before reaching a checkpoint / gate access area. Full sized Hescos can stop even large trucks from crashing your gates.

(Skill Level: Intermediate)

Gabions or Hesco containers are effective cover and barriers.

Razor Wire and Barbed Wire: Barbed wire is available at any home or farm supply store. For instance, when this was written, an 80 Rod (440 yards) spool of barbed wire was $50 at Tractor Supply. The down side to barbed wire is that it is not self supporting. You will need engineer stakes (T-posts), wooden posts, or something like the hedgehog we discussed previously. The upside is the cost effectiveness and versatility.

Keep in mind, you will need a post driver or a sledgehammer to drive in T-posts. A sledgehammer will work but for one or two, but if you are going to drive several of these, you should invest in or borrow a dedicated post driver.

Engineering stakes or "T" posts can be found at hardware, farm, and home stores.

Razor wire comes in rolls and is self-supporting. You can stretch out a roll of razor wire and it stands up. The diameter of the rolls of razor wire will vary from 12 inches all the way up to 36 inches. On the commercial market, 18 inch rolls of razor wire seem to be the most common. Like barbed wire, you can order and pick up razor wire at home and farm stores. You can even get it from Walmart or Amazon. Remember to purchase a few pairs of thick *"Wire Handling Gloves"*. Your hands will thank you.

If you are having a tough time finding dedicated wire handling gloves, at very least, secure thick leather palm gloves. Welders gloves can work for wire. If you cannot find either of these, get some genuine cowhide leather work gloves.

(Skill Level: Intermediate)

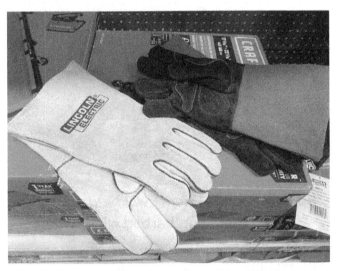

A thick set of Welders Gloves will protect your hands.

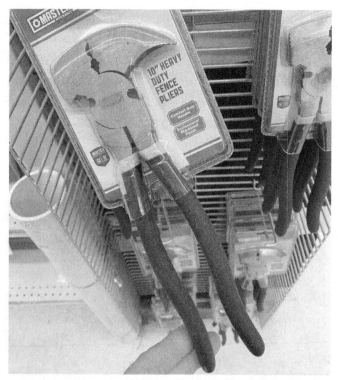

Special "Fence Pliers" will help you when installing barbed wire.

Barbed and razor wire are primarily used to deny/restrict access to people on foot. Yes, a car or truck could drive over/through wire, but the tires won't last very long. Imagine the rushing mob scenario. How do you slow down fifty armed looters with only a few men? Even in a deadly force situation, you will find it difficult at best to address forty or fifty threats, all at once.

Regardless of how motivated, cracked up, or angry a mob might be, they are not going to be happy campers when they run into triple thick rows of razor wire. Even if they attempt to breach the razor wire with ladders, discarded house doors, or lumber, that will take time and it also creates a funnel point on to which the defenders can focus. Razor wire can be cut with heavy duty tools, but that is not something the average thugs are likely to have. Cutting through barbed or razor wire is again a time consuming affair, giving the defenders time to react to the threat.

Barbed wire fences slow people down and inconvenience them. Razor wire fences rip them up and make them miserable. Either a barbed wire or razor wire fence can be put up to restrict access and to funnel people toward a single opening.

**Barbed wire is common in rural
environments and readily available.**

Barbed/Razor Wire Tangle-Foot: If you have
an open field or area that you need to cover
and restrict access to, you can create a
tangle-foot barrier by using short (2 to 3 foot)
wooden stakes and either barbed wire or razor
wire. The stakes should be robust, at least
2"x2" thick. *Note: you should have a 1-3
pound hammer to drive the stakes.

For a barbed wire tangle-foot, pound your
stakes in the ground at least six to eight inches
and create a grid pattern with the space
between the stakes set at one or two paces.
Wrap the barbed wire around the stakes so

that it is approximately on foot off of the ground. (If you have an industrial staple gun that might speed up the process). Should the field be overgrown with grass, all the better, the enemy will not see the tangle-food until they are stuck in it. Ditto for snow. If you anticipate very deep and hard packed snow the tangle-foot will lose its effectiveness, however, unless your enemy is using snowshoes or cross country skis, deep snow will slow them down considerably.

Speaking of snow. Heavy snow cover, that which completely covers the grass, is a benefit to the defender. Intruders and prowlers cannot help but to leave tracks in the snow that are easy to notice and identify. Also, snow cover reflects moonlight and starlight making it much easier for defenders to spot intruders under cover of darkness.

Snow cover also enhances the use of night vision and helps to extend its useful range. Ditto thermal imagers although for a different reason. The heat signatures from humans stand out even more so than they would in the warmer times of the year.

To construct a razor wire tangle-foot, you will create the same grid pattern with wooden stakes. The benefit of razor wire is that it is self-supporting. You will simply need to stretch it out and drop it over the top of the stakes.

Your tangle-foot should be a minimum ten yards deep to prevent the enemy from trying to jump over it or to breach it by throwing ladders, doors, plywood, etc, on top of it. If you really want to be slick, you can create a "kill zone" by putting down ten yards of tangle-foot leaving 20 to 30 yards of open space and then another 10 yards of tangle-foot. The enemy cannot advance quickly nor can they retreat quickly once they are between the two sets of razor wire tanglefoot.

As they could when confronted with a fence, a person who moves slowly and deliberately, under cover of darkness or fog, can try to step or climb over your barrier. For this reason, it is a good idea to mix tripwire alarms (audible and flare) in with your tangle-foot.

(Skill Level: Intermediate)

Razor wire is an extremely effective deterrent for intruders.

Trip Flares and Noisemakers

Tripwire alarms have been around a long, long time. The Vietnam War is largely responsible for popularizing trip flares or tripwire audible alarms. These devices are simple concepts. You have a spring-loaded striker held in place by a pin attached to a length of thin wire or even fishing line. When "tripped" the pin comes out, the striker hits a primer and either a flare launches or a super-loud, blank cartridge goes "Boom!"

Imagine a perfectly still, quiet night. It's 0230 and your night watch sentry is struggling to stay awake. Out of nowhere, Boom! The sound of a 12 gauge shotgun blank shatters the night. Or, there is a heavily used walking trail that leads to your property. Two hundred yards from your fence line you mount trip flares across the trail. Again, the middle of night; bang, woosh, a bright red flare streaks through the blackened sky. Bingo, someone or some ones is/are busted.

At present, 12 gauge marine flares and 12 gauge blank cartridges are the easiest to find for the non-military person. There are several companies that offer ready made "bear alarms" or "sonic alarms" and they are priced modestly.

Tripwire flares or noise alarms are best utilized by placing them across likely avenues of approach. They also act as a force multiplier because you will not be able to be everywhere at all times. Trip wires can also be attached to rarely used gates, side entrances, etc. Also, they can be attached to things you might need to store outside, but a thief might want to steal; portable propane tanks come immediately to mind.

Naturally, all of the team members need to be aware of the placement of tripwire alarms. They won't injure them, but they might cause involuntary bladder evacuation and then your surprise is ruined. If a friendly or an enemy activates a tripwire alarm you will need to relocate it. Also, from an OpSec (Operational Security) standpoint, you will want to install your tripwire alarms when prying eyes cannot observe you. This may mean installing them after the sun has set.

If you cannot afford or find a ready supply of trip wire alarms, a cheap solution is to attach empty soup cans to wire fences and tangle-foot. If the wire is pulled or stepped on the can makes noise. The downside to this is a windy environment. On a windy night, you will experience quite the glockenspiel concert.

(Skill Level: Beginner)

**Tripwire Alarm w 12 gauge blank round.
(photo courtesy of FithOps.com)**

As I was preparing this book to go to print, FithOps released a new tripwire activated product that they are calling the "O.C. Intruder-Buster". The unit is mounted as you would any tripwire alarm, except for this one, when the pin is pulled, a canister full of O.C.

(Oleoresin Capsicum), better known as pepper spray, is released into the area. It should be apparent that such a device would be most effective indoors where the suspect could not just run away from the burning O.C. Storage sheds, warehouses, infrequently used buildings like cabins, etc. all would seem to be good candidates for this product.

For the uninitiated, O.C. / pepper spray is less-than-lethal, but it is an extremely effective subject control tool. The suspect won't die, they will just think they are dying until it wears off in an hour or so.

Naturally, just with any type of alarm system or tripwire device, you want to be absolutely sure that all friendly personnel with the need to know are aware of these devices. A negligent pepper spray discharge won't kill them but it will make for a very uncomfortable day.

Before we continue, I'm sure that at least one person who picks up this book will say, "I heard that pepper spray doesn't work on..." fill in the blank. I have been carrying and using OC since around 1994. During that time I have sprayed in excess of three hundred humans and animals who had it coming. I can remember a total of two (2) humans who were not affected to the point of incapacitation. They were mildly annoyed. I can assure you that 99 percent of burglars and thieves who find themselves inside of a cloud of OC will notice it and immediately regret their bad choice. Who knows, that might just be the moment they turn their life around.

**O.C. Intruder-Buster, a tripwire activated intruder deterrent device.
(photo courtesy of FithOps.com)**

Natural Barriers

For thousands of years, men have used natural barriers as impediments to keep their enemies at bay. Mountains, deserts, rivers, and even oceans have been effective deterrents or at least greatly hampered attackers for centuries.

Consider where you live, where your community is located and whether or not there are natural barriers. How many highways lead to your city? Do you have an interstate system that is in your city or very close by? Such a highway system makes travel super convenient. However, it also makes accessing your city easy for those who would wish to descend upon your community and take what you have from you.

Many of you might be thinking, "Well, this is where I live. There is nothing I can do to change the fact that two interstate highways intersect in my city." That is true enough, but you need to think about what that means from a security standpoint.

Water as a Barrier

When discussing ways to deny access to your city, community, neighborhood or just a large piece of property, water as a barrier is a topic that many readers might be thinking about. Afterall, moats around castles were effective barriers for hundreds of years.

Let's consider the idea of using a ditch system as a potential barrier around a large piece or property. Naturally, a backhoe or other heavy equipment would make the job easier. The idea of a dozen men with shovels digging ditches is rather antiquated.

A ditch system will naturally only be an effective barrier for foot traffic if it is filled with water, preferably moving water not still or stagnant water. Any ditch that is more than a couple of feet deep will be an impediment to normal vehicle traffic, full or empty.

If you have to use a modern moat to keep unwanted people from getting onto your property, it will need to be deep and full of water. A constant reliable water source, such as a river or reservoir, will need to be tapped.

Occasional rainwater or melted snow is not going to keep your barrier ditch filled.

If you decide to dig a barrier ditch, but it is empty, what you have instead created is a trench system that could be used by intruders to cover their movement and presence. Also, in an extreme case, the man made trench could be used as cover by hostile persons to fire at your friendly personnel. That is definitely a downside.

Additionally, while we are on the subject, when you are setting up your community / neighborhood defense, you will need to conduct a site assessment from the outside looking in.

Site Survey/Assessment

You and those working with you should go outside of the area you wish to secure and look at it as though you were bad guys attempting to get in undetected. Keep in mind, you will need to conduct this type of risk assessment or site survey both day and night.

Are there natural depressions, thickly wooded areas, overgrown fields, etc. that would allow intruders to get into your community before you could detect them? At night, are the areas where the street lights or security lights don't cover? Could a person simply navigate under the cover of deep shadows or darkness?

When you find such problem areas, you will need to have a solution. Do you need more light? Or, will you be equipping night security personnel with night vision devices?

I have conducted a great many site surveys for clients in need of executive protection. Regarding security during hours of darkness you need to light up the entire property to be secured or you revert to complete blackout.

Partial light, where some parts of the property are illuminated but others are bathed in shadow is the worst situation. The reason for this should be obvious, but allow me a moment.

When the property is partly illuminated, intruders will just stick to the dark part or shadows. The eyes of the security will adjust to the light and it will be difficult to see in the shadows without handheld illumination.

Also, if the security element has night vision devices, hard light / shadow contrasts make it difficult to use such equipment effectively or to its full potential.

I have been involved in scenarios where both of the aforementioned nocturnal solutions were applied. Some clients will install additional lights or even rent/purchase diesel powered flood light towers to fill in the gaps.

Additionally, I have worked in situations where the entire property was blacked out and security either allowed their eyes to adjust or they had night vision devices.

The blackout situation was often used when the threat of sniper fire was an issue. Of course, you need to hope your adversaries do not also have night vision capabilities.

Whatever you decide, it is better to have these conversations and make decision during times of calm, not during the middle of an emergency or a crisis.

Note from Nic Orr: If at any time you might think this preparation is excessive or paranoid, consider the option of having your neighborhood overrun by fifty to a hundred armed thugs. Think about watching your family run crying from your burning house. Imagine your wife and daughter being repeatedly raped while your dead body grows cold twenty feet away. Now, get back to work preparing your neighborhood and your team.

Chapter 2   Fire Bases

by Nicholas Orr

Fire support bases or simply "fire bases" are forward areas occupied and secured by friendly personnel in a hostile environment. The fire base was popularized during Vietnam and the concept was rejuvenated during our recent involvement in Afghanistan. In addition to providing support fire from mortars and artillery, fire bases also can launch reactionary forces to support other fire bases, security and combat patrols and offensive operations.

While I don't anticipate that your cul-de-sac will possess 81mm mortars or 155 howitzers (artillery is a beautiful thing) you can support other communities and neighborhoods in your area if mutual aid agreements are made between them. This is where solid community leadership comes into play.

Long before the balloon goes up or the lights go out, take your pick of metaphors, good people in neighboring communities need to have open lines of communication with one another. Ask your local Sheriff about mutual aid agreements. I would be willing to bet that your county Sheriff has a mutual aid agreement with all of the other counties that border yours. It is not all that complex, these agencies simply agree, before a crisis or emergency, that they will come to each other's aid if and when they are called upon to do so.

Speaking of law enforcement officials. You will need to take a hard look and evaluate your local Chief of Police or County Sheriff. In the United States of America today we have two camps regarding the heads of law enforcement agencies. In one camp we have Chiefs and Sheriffs who believe that citizens should be armed to defend themselves against felonious attack.

However, there are many in the other camp. There are Sheriffs and Chiefs in the nation who have been bought off by the anti-freedom, liberal left and they are vocal "gun control" proponents. These men have deliberately defecated on the oaths they took to "support and uphold the Constitution of the United States of America."

Amendment Two says "Shall not be infringed", it does not say, "Any reasonable disarmament that is currently popular". If you have an anti-freedom/anti-liberty Chief or Sheriff, it is a safe bet that they would rather you call 9-1-1 and sit quietly for "the professionals" to arrive than for you to take up arms for the defense of your community.

Long before the emergency or crisis occurs, you need to know whether you can count on your senior law enforcement official to either support you or to seek to disarm you. Either way it is better to know before than after.

Of course, the good news is that a Sheriff is elected every four years. A Police Chief is not an elected official, but the Mayor and City Council who hired him or her are subject to election. If you have an anti-freedom / gun control chief, you can let your mayor know that until he or she is gone, you are going to campaign for their (mayor's) opponent.

There is no reason why your community, particularly if you live in a rural area where towns and villages are separated by miles of open country, cannot engage in a mutual aid compact with others. If your towns and villages are spread out and separated by farm and ranch land, I would suspect that your small village police department already has a mutual aid agreement with the police department in the next town over and the sheriff's office.

The Fire Base concept is not limited to small towns or villages. In rural areas, privately owned farms and ranches can and should have mutual aid compacts between one another. In large metropolitan areas, neighborhoods can have compacts with other neighborhoods. Cul de sac communities with their neighboring community.

Communication and preparation are the two most important keywords regarding mutual aid compacts. During the chaos of a widespread emergency or a crisis, it is going to be much more difficult to sit down with your neighbors and have a calm, thoughtful discussion regarding disaster preparedness. These conversations need to be had BEFORE the crisis occurs not after.

Also, during the communication phase, it is important that all parties involved are engaged in preparation operations and training for their people. For instance, let's say that "Community A" has been diligently putting up ample food stores, participating in disaster or crisis management training, and has armed security people ready to go.

Then you have "Community B" that has engaged in none of the above. Community B people like to say that they are not "paranoid" and that they can't imagine things getting "that bad". How are the people of Community A going to feel about running to the aid of Community B?

We used to read our children stories and fables about the importance of work and preparedness. Do you remember the fable of the Ants and the Grasshopper? The grasshopper fiddled all summer long while the ants worked. How about the story of "The Little Red Hen" and how no one wanted to help her make the bread. For those who were shortchanged in school, I have printed it here.

The Little Red Hen by Bob Bullock 1961

One day as the Little Red Hen was scratching in a field, she found a grain of wheat.
"This wheat should be planted," she said. "Who will plant this grain of wheat?"
"Not I," said the Duck.
"Not I," said the Cat.

"Not I," said the Dog.

"Then I will," said the Little Red Hen. And she did.

Soon the wheat grew to be tall and yellow.

"The wheat is ripe," said the Little Red Hen.

"Who will cut the wheat?"

"Not I," said the Duck.

"Not I," said the Cat.

"Not I," said the Dog.

"Then I will," said the Little Red Hen. And she did.

When the wheat was cut, the Little Red Hen said, "Who will thresh the wheat?"

"Not I," said the Duck.

"Not I," said the Cat.

"Not I," said the Dog.

"Then I will," said the Little Red Hen. And she did.

When the wheat was threshed, the Little Red Hen said, "Who will take this wheat to the mill?"

"Not I," said the Duck.

"Not I," said the Cat.

"Not I," said the Dog.

"Then I will," said the Little Red Hen. And she did.

She took the wheat to the mill and had it ground into flour. Then she said, "Who will make this flour into bread?"

"Not I," said the Duck.

"Not I," said the Cat.
"Not I," said the Dog.
"Then I will," said the Little Red Hen. And she did.
She made and baked the bread. Then she said, "Who will eat this bread?"
"Oh! I will," said the Duck.
"And I will," said the Cat.
"And I will," said the Dog.
"No, No!" said the Little Red Hen. "I will do that." And she did.

Don't laugh. This is not an oversimplification as some of you might believe. Those who put in all of the work and the effort to be prepared are going to have a very natural distrust or lack of respect for those who did not put in the work or the effort to get ready for a disaster. Remember, we are dealing with real people here, not some notional social experiment in a college class.

Consider the Proverbs of King Solomon; Chapter 10 verses 4 and 5, *"Lazy hands make for poverty, but diligent hands bring wealth. He who gathers crops in summer is a prudent son, but he who sleeps during harvest is a disgraceful son."*

Unfortunately, for at least a generation, we have bred and raised people that have been convinced that they should have anything that they *want,* regardless of whether or not they worked for it or earned it; because everything should be *fair.* This entitlement mentality combined with apathy makes for woefully unprepared people and communities.

If your community, neighborhood, ranch or village is going to have a mutual aid agreement with other such entities, it is critical that everyone involved shares the same serious interest in being prepared and self-sufficient or resilient if you prefer that term. Those who have worked and saved and prepared are going to have a hard time feeling sorry for those who "fiddled" during the harvest and have nothing to show for it.

For years I have heard people say, "If things ever get really bad, I'm coming to your house." My friend, James Yeager, got sick of hearing such statements. He began to respond to the people who said *I'm coming to your house* by saying, "You had better show up with a fucking truckload of food and water."

The First Step

If your community has not taken the first step toward unity or at very least mutual agreement regarding how to prepare and react to a crisis or a disaster, you need to get on that and get on it quickly.

Those who have their eyes open and have paid attention to history and what is currently happening in our world might want to begin by setting up some type of "Disaster Preparation". At such a gathering you would be tempted to dive right into "The End of the World as We Know It" scenarios.

I would advise against that, at least in the beginning. Most humans, by nature, do not want to think about the end of the world or even localized crises or catastrophe. Many, if not most, believe that troubles are fleeting or, and I have heard this ad nauseum, "I don't think it will ever get *that* bad".

The suggestion that I have for a first step in regards to a neighborhood or community coming together is a neighborhood cookout, pot luck dinner, or pancake breakfast at the local rec center. Engage in activity that is not deadly serious or "end of the world". This should be your first step.

If you are doing a community gathering at a local park, strongly consider hiring a local band to play uplifting music for the people as they eat their hot dogs and hamburgers. Organize games for the kids and get some local businesses to donate prizes of some type.

I would not even bring up the community security and crisis preparation subject at the first gathering. Let's face it, in our modern world most people might see their neighbors coming and going, but they don't even know most of their names.

The goal of the first community gathering is to get the neighbors out of their houses and have them actually meet each other face to face. This is a far better strategy than waiting for an emergency or disaster and then attempting to get strangers to work together.

Chapter 3 Home Fortress

by Jeff Kirkham

Although our goal is to keep the fight as far from our home as possible, we need to consider how to fortify our individual homes. During this chapter we will consider this in detail. The following advice can be used during times of peace and times of conflict.

The more difficult and time consuming your house is to break into, the more a potential criminal will want to move on to easier houses. The goal is to make it a pain in the ass for someone to break into your house, or, at the very least, make your house look like it is a pain in the ass to break into.

According to the FBI, most burglaries take place between 6 am and 6 pm in the summer months when there is maximum daylight! Consider that for a moment.

Let's break it down statistically and take a look at the situation. Here are the top seven common points of access criminals use to invade homes:

- **34% – Through the front door**
- **23% – Through the first-floor windows (bad guys love them!)**
- **22% – Through a back door**
- **9% – Through the garage**
- **6% – Through unlocked storage areas**
- **4% – Through basement door or window**
- **2% – Through the second-floor window**

Based on these statistics, the most important places to fortify are the front and back doors. Next in line would be all the first-floor windows.

Locks

-Did you change your locks or codes when you moved in?

-Who has keys or knows the code?

-Some of the easiest locks to pick are cheap, mass produced door locks.

-Properly installed quality locks are the foundation of security!

Doors

-Lock and secure your friggin' doors!

-Use deadbolts (electric deadbolts are great! They self lock.)

-Solid sturdy doors are a must and worth every penny

-Solid sturdy door frames go with the sturdy door

-3 inch deck/grabber screws in hinges and bolt plate increase security by a factor of 10.

-Lock your screen doors.

-Have security bars inside the door frame.

-Use a door wedge to hinder forceable entry.

-Privacy film on windows next to doors so they can't see in but you can see out.

-Remote security cameras with video capability are a great, inexpensive option (Ring).

-Lock the door from your garage into your house!

-Bar or bolt for sliding glass doors.

-Hang a bell on your door, super simple early warning that someone has just used that door.

Windows

-Lock your friggin windows!

-PVC pipe in the frame to bar windows and sliding glass doors.

-Drill a hole in window frames and use a nail to block windows from opening or only allow part way opening.

-Secondary lock device to allow partial opening but still secure.

-Plexiglas/clear polycarbonate is super strong and cheap. Use it to armor your windows.

-Solar film will slow break-ins down, as well as keep prying eyes away and give advance warning of a break in.

-Security film is probably the best option here. It won't stop them but it will slow them down considerably and make them create a lot of noise.

-Have sturdy frames in place.

-Old school bars and decorative iron-work.

-Use your blinds and curtains to keep prying eyes from seeing the interior of your house.

-Close blinds and curtains every night.

Signage

-Post signs around the property saying you have a dog, a video camera, and alarms. Don't be sneaky with these things; overt presentation keeps them away.

-Even if you have none of the above, make any would-be intruder think that you do.

-Use fake video cameras; they are cheap and will make burglars think twice.

Bushes and Thorns

-Every rose has a thorn, and they look good too!

-Thick thorny bushes under windows.

-These bushes hurt like hell and keep prying eyes at a distance.

-Blackberry and raspberry bushes work well and provide food too.

-Cacti and mesquite have been used for centuries as fences and barriers from unwanted intruders.

Lights

-Flood lights (hard wired to house)

-Solar lights (easy to install, inexpensive, put them anywhere)

-Motion detecting lights (hard wired or solar)

-Exterior and interior lights set on timers when you are away.

-TV set on a timer when you are away.

Alarms

-Door bell cameras/alarms are essential.

-Self-monitored or third-party monitored alarms that have speakers that inform the intruder the police are on the way.

-Full-fledged alarm systems that contact police

-Loud sirens that go off if alarm is tripped

-Inexpensive door chimes and sirens that are available at hardware stores.

Security (Surveillance) Cameras

-Don't be intimidated by the installation. It is now easy and intuitive to set up a camera system that is robust, wireless, and runs for weeks on batteries allowing you to put cameras up anywhere you have wi-fi access.

-High-end monitored cameras are now relatively inexpensive.

-Inexpensive cameras can be purchased at most hardware stores, COSTCO, etc.

-Fake cameras will slow down a would-be intruder. Note: The bad guys don't know if a camera is monitored or not. They just see cameras and will likely move on to an easier target.

Dogs

-Over and over again we hear from criminals that dogs (especially big dogs) are the #1 deterrent - they do not want to tangle with a loud, potentially violent dog.

-Even little yapping dogs are great for early warning.

-If you don't have a dog, have a sign that you do. Add visible food and water bowls that look like a dog lives there.

Fences

-These have been around since time immemorial but can work both ways.

-Fences block snooping looky loos from getting close to your house where they can see who and what you have in your home.

-Fences create a stand off from your home if someone is inside your fence they are trespassing and it's hard for them to say they made a mistake or did not know.

-Fences can create a false sense of security.

-Be careful since fences can also hide the nefarious activities of someone on the other side of the fence (pre-operational surveillance, damage to the fence, efforts to scale the fence.)

Safes

-Keep valuables in a metal safe that is impossible to move.

-Conceal the safe so that it is not easy to detect.

-Have multiple safes in your house (wall safes are inexpensive and easy to install).

-If traveling, lock your car keys up in a wall safe.

-A safe will increase the time an intruder is in the house, creating more time for you to react or for the police to arrive.

Garages

-Do not leave your garage door open. Open garage doors allow people to see what you have and to scope out possible ways to enter.

-If you are traveling, unplug your garage door opener.

-If you are traveling, use the manual lock on the garage door.

-Replace the pull cord handle with a knot or ball to avoid "fishing attacks," where people access the cord from the outside in order to open the garage.

-Don't leave your garage door opener in your vehicle if it is parked outside.

-Do not leave your car keys in your vehicle even when it is in your garage.

-Lock the door from your garage to the inside of your house.

-Have a solid door between the garage and your house.

-Do not leave keys sitting out if you are on vacation or traveling (put in a safe or hide).

Vehicles

-Never leave the keys in the car (ignition or otherwise) even for a short period of time.

-Keep the doors locked.

-Keep the windows rolled all the way up.

-Never leave valuables in the car. If you have to leave important items in the car, hide them from view.

-Put any car items in the trunk or back seat hidden.

-Cover any items in the car to obscure what they are.
-Never leave a phone or computer in your car.

-Any tools should be hidden or in the trunk of a car.

-Ensure that the spare tire is inflated and tools are in the trunk.

Neighborhood and Neighbors

-Know what normal looks like in your neighborhood.

-Know what normal sounds like in your neighborhood.

-Make friends with your neighbors (or at least know who they are and have a way to communicate with them).

-Know who the neighborhood kids are and where they live.

-Know the different vehicles that belong in your neighborhood.

-That nosey neighbor may be your best friend when they call the police because someone was tapping on your window with a hammer.

-Neighborhood watch programs, even informal ones, work and friends watching out for friends is the basis of security.

-Post a Neighborhood Watch sign throughout your area, even if you don't have one.

Leaving your home for travel or vacation

-If you are not home, make sure that one of your friends or neighbors has keys to your house and goes inside every couple days to check on it (break ins, water leaks, etc.).

-Make sure that your newspaper gets picked up as well as packages or any other items visible from the front of the house.

-Make sure that your mail gets picked up.

-If you are gone for an extended period of time, hire a neighbor kid to cut your grass, take out your trash cans, etc.

-Have a neighbor kid shovel the snow on your driveway if you are going to be away.

Shredder

-Shred all personal documents.

-Shred all paper that has a name and address on it (even magazine covers).

-Shred all membership or club documents.

-Shred all credit cards, member cards, credit card applications, etc.

-Shred all applications for loans or auto loan junk mail.

-If a shredder is not available then tear it into small pieces.

-Shred your hotel card keys (don't turn them back in).

Cyber

- Do not name your wifi router something personalized. This name is visible to anyone in range and will identify which network belongs to you.

- Create a new password for your router/modem. Do not use the one provided by the wireless provider or the manufacturer.

- Ensure your wi-fi password is complex and unique. Do not use the same password for other accounts.

- Do not store your wifi password somewhere obvious. Use a password manager or vault.

-Have a guest wifi for your house with a separate password.

-All smart devices in the home must be password protected.

-Pick a long phrase that is easy for you to remember as your password, for example: RomeFell&PoliticiansRGreedy!12345.

- Regularly update your smart devices for patches and updated security settings, even the benign ones like your refrigerator, Smart thermostats, and wi-fi enabled TVs.

Email

-Never click on a link from someone you do not know.

-Never open an attachment without a virus scan.

-Ensure your computer has antivirus software.

-Do a thorough review of all financial emails before opening/clicking, as phishing scammers are becoming increasingly savvy on their ability to generate realistic fakes.

Social Media

-Set all personal accounts to "private".

-Do not post vacation/travel photos online until you are back home.

-Never post personal data/information online, this includes addresses, birth dates, anniversary dates, etc.

-Avoid providing information on social media that ties to information frequently used by banks to confirm your identity, such as the make/model of your first car, the street you grew up on, and your best friend's name. There are a lot of funny memes that ask you to comment with this info- they are scams seeking to obtain your personal information.

Phone

-Ensure your phone has antivirus software.

-Always password protect your phone. Your phone should lock-out after a short period (30 seconds to 1 minute) of no use. Biometrics are a great way to secure your phone. At minimum, use a pin or pattern.

Chapter 4 Tactics

By Nicholas Orr

Tactics, definition: skillful manipulation of time, distance, and circumstance, in such a manner that you get a turn, but your adversary does not.

As we progress and examine numerous tactics, consider the above definition and whether or not it applies to the tactic of which we are discussing.

Buying material, building fences, putting up signs and filling sandbags are all important, but we must understand and use sound tactics when employing our barriers and barricades. When all else is equal; if your side has guns and their side has guns, it is the side that employs the best and most effective tactics that will win the battle and the war.

Temporary Solutions

You must keep in mind that all cover or barricades are temporary solutions. Given enough time, the enemy will always find a way to defeat your cover and barricades or get around them. You cannot just build sandbag walls, stretch out razor wire and then wander off hoping the enemy will be dissuaded. Check points must be manned by armed men. Routine and frequent security patrols must be conducted. If you want to keep the monsters and vermin away from your wives and children, this is part of the price you will need to pay.

In addition to **road blocks, check points, and security patrols**, another weapon in your arsenal needs to be some form of **overwatch**. In short, you need to find the highest position or a few positions in your area of operation and put men with magnified optics and rifles in/on them. The men in the overwatch position act as lookouts and communicate to the men on the ground giving them warning of approaching threats.

The men in overwatch positions will naturally have rifles with high powered, optical sights to engage deadly threats to the community. Overwatch is one of those jobs that requires a leader to be absolutely sure that the most qualified people are manning these posts. You cannot be on the ground worried and wondering if the guys on overwatch are sleeping. Also, you must have one hundred percent confidence in the marksmanship skills of said men. These jobs will generally go to well-trained, combat veterans first and police sharpshooters secondly. If you have no vets or SWAT guys on your team, put some skilled and experienced hunters up there.

Keep in mind, the bad guys will employ snipers too. During the first few days after the collapse of New Orleans, post-Katrina, bad guys frequently climbed up on roofs and parking garages to take pot shots at targets of opportunity. The enemy might decide to take out your check point guards with a sniper of their own. How are you going to deal with that?

If your area of operation has little to offer in the way of elevated platforms, a skilled engineer with the right materials (telephone poles) can build you a watch tower. My advice is that if you build one watchtower that you build at least two. If there is only one tower, the enemy will know where to focus. If you have more than one, you can alternate watches or even set up decoy positions.

Considering that your manpower might be stretched thin, it is not a bad idea to build more sandbag bunkers than you have men to fill them. Put dummies with BB guns or airsoft rifles in them. Of course, you need to mix it up. Switch out the decoys with live shooters frequently to keep the enemy spies on their toes.

Bear in mind, if you have done a good job securing your neighborhood, the enemy will conduct recon on you before they just come charging in. Think this is a paranoid fantasy? There are cities and suburban neighborhoods in America and across the world that are being terrorized by thugs right now as these words are typed. The residents are cowering like pathetic sheep behind locked doors praying that they don't get murdered or burned out with fire bombs.

Make Hard Targets

We need to consider and understand the mentality of the thief and the bully. The majority of criminals are lazy and opportunistic. They are looking for the easiest score that presents the least amount of danger to them. Bullies are not people who are looking for a fight. Bullies are those who want to impose their will upon you minus any resistance on your part.

Mobs of looters and rioters tend to be a combination of criminals and bullies. They want to impose their will upon others, steal whatever they desire, and do it all without resistance from their intended victims. Consider the lesson of the Rooftop Koreans during the 1992 LA Riots.

After riots broke out in Los Angeles, the violence rapidly spread to the surrounding areas. When it became obvious that the police were overwhelmed and could not respond to individual calls for help, criminal looters and rioters took advantage of the situation. Korean business owners armed themselves and took to the rooftops to drive off the gangs of criminals descending on their community. The Korean citizens of Los Angeles made their neighborhood a hard target. Those who preyed upon them did so at great risk to their lives. Realizing that the people were fighting back, the vast majority of the criminal looters and rioters decided to go somewhere else and pick on someone else. This is the kind of situation you are attempting to create in your neighborhood / community.

When the thieves, looters, rioters, whatever, look at your neighborhood, you want them to see a well-prepared and defended community. You want these vermin to decide that there are better/easier victims somewhere else. Your tactics must be up to speed to the point where you can deal with a variety of threats.

3 Threat Types

Many years ago, Paul Markel of Student of the Gun explained the three (3) types of threats posed by violent felons or armed criminals. We will consider these and how this information applies to a civil emergency or riot situation.

A Type 1 attacker, when met with resistance in the form of a firearm, will surrender or flee out of a sense of self-preservation even though they have received no injury.

A Type 2 attacker will flee or surrender only AFTER they have received an injury. This injury is not immediately life threatening, but it *hurts*. Career criminals use guns and see guns all the time, they do not fear the sight of a gun. However, the reality of a physical injury may cause them to withdraw or surrender and beg for medical attention.

A Type 3 attacker will not cease their assault, regardless of the defender being armed or sustaining some type of injury to themselves. The bad guys in the 1986 Miami Shootout and the 1997 North Hollywood Bank Robbery are likely the most famous examples of Type 3 attackers. The Type 3 attacker will NOT stop until they have received physical damage to the point that their body can no longer respond to the commands from their brain.

Both the Type 1 and Type 2 attackers surrender or flee based upon a *psychological* decision, they make the mental choice to cease their attack. The Type 3 threat cannot be stopped psychologically, only *physiologically.* It is only after sustaining sufficient physiological damage that the Type 3 attacker will stop their deadly assault.

The good news is that there are far more Type 1 and Type 2 attackers in the world than Type 3. The bad news is that when faced with a deadly force attack, the defender will not know what type of threat they are facing until AFTER the fight has concluded. The moral of the story is that you must be mentally and physically prepared to deal with all three types of attackers at any moment in time.

Checkpoints and Roadblocks

Often the terms "checkpoints" and "roadblocks" are used interchangeably. This is not necessarily a bad thing, however, we must understand the difference between completely shutting down traffic/travel on a road and restricting access to only approved personnel/vehicles.

Roadblocks in the strictest sense, completely shut down an avenue of travel and prevent vehicle traffic. To a combat engineer, the best roadblock is accomplished with an ample amount of high explosives. I recall during demo training, my team blew a hole in a dirt road that was large enough to swallow up a deuce-and-a-half truck. Removing bridges with high explosives is an effective combat engineer tactic, but it is a rather extreme choice.

An effective roadblock can be set up using industrial sized concrete barriers, this will put thousands of pounds in the way of oncoming traffic. Steel 55 gallon drums filled with sand can be used, ditto Hesco barriers. Keep in mind that steel drums filled with water can be shot full of holes and drained in minutes.

In wooded areas, hasty roadblocks can be set up by felling trees in the right direction. The tree solution is fast, but it will be temporary, and it only works if you have conveniently grown or staged trees. Also, mother nature can be tapped and roadways can be deliberately flooded in order to make them impassible. The point is to use what you have available.

One of the most common reasons to set up a semi-permanent roadblock is to force traffic onto a road where a checkpoint has been established. Such action provides you with environmental control.

Checkpoints are set up on roadways in order to slow and stop vehicles in order to determine who should be allowed entry and who should be turned away. Checkpoint locations will require dedicated and deliberate planning regarding location.

The Turnaround First, you must have an area that is wide enough for a turnaround. The purpose of the checkpoint is to restrict access to your community to those with a genuine need to be there. This means by default that you are likely going to have to turn away people whom you have determined do not need to be in your neighborhood. Unless you want to create a nightmarish traffic jam, you must build in a turnaround area so the vehicles you dismiss can go away. No, you do not want drivers attempting to execute 3-point turns in front of your checkpoint. Such a situation will rapidly become a shitshow.

Serpentine Barriers In order to slow approaching vehicles to a crawl and prevent them from blasting through your checkpoint, you will need at a minimum three heavy duty barriers staggered in a serpentine pattern. These barriers should be spaced approximately 1 and ½ car lengths apart. This is enough to let vehicles move through, slowly.

Warning Signs Before vehicles reach your barriers there needs to be signage advising them to "PREPARE to STOP" or "SLOW DOWN", "Checkpoint Ahead" also works. You need to give drivers at least 100 yards or more warning so they can decelerate. Remember, a good percent of your customers at the checkpoint will be good guys. We don't want the good people needlessly crashing into our barriers.

Guard shack / Bunker Your checkpoint will need to have some kind of guard shack or structure for your men to get out of the weather when there is no traffic present. Additionally, this structure needs to be reinforced so that it will provide cover from small arms fire. We must be prepared to deal with people who do not have our best interests at heart.

During checkpoint traffic stops, only one man (contact man) will leave the cover of the guard shack, at least one other man will provide cover support (cover man). The guard shack should be off to the side of the road and angled so as to allow the cover man a clear shot on the stopped vehicle. Depending on the volume of traffic that is anticipated, your checkpoint might need to be manned by several armed men. This is naturally situational dependent.

If the occupants of the vehicle produce weapons or attempt to run the checkpoint, the contact man needs to hit the ground, and fast, so the cover man can do his job. The cover man should be sufficiently armed with a weapon that can produce volume fire. Uncle Jim might be a "crack shot" with his bolt-action "-06", but that is not the correct tool for providing cover fire.

When the vehicle has been cleared to pass, the final barriers (spike board, jack rock chain, LE spike strips) are pulled out of the way. If your checkpoint has steady traffic you might consider some kind of barrier swing arm / gate.

A serious question that you must ask yourselves as members of a community security force is; how important is restricting traffic? While this might seem rhetorical, I assure you that it is not.

Before you set up a roadblock or checkpoint, consider who is going to be manning it or whether anyone will be.

To be fair some roadblocks don't need to be manned 24/7. If you put concrete barriers, weighing thousands of pounds (a 10 ft. concrete "Jersey" barrier weighs 4000 lbs), across a roadway, you don't really need to worry that the local teenagers are going to push them out of the way.

Regarding checkpoints where you will be restricting both vehicle and foot traffic, you must be prepared to man them day and night.

Consider the following checklist of questions before you set up a traffic checkpoint.

☐ Do you have the manpower to do so? You need at least 4 capable men, 6 is better.

☐ Will your checkpoint be open to traffic day and night or will you shut the road down at sunset?

☐ If your checkpoint is open 24 hours, do you have floodlights, a power generator, and ample fuel? You cannot have a blacked out checkpoint and you cannot rely on streetlights alone.

☐ Will your neighborhood security team, or perhaps the Chief or Sheriff, set an after dark curfew?

☐ Who is going to enforce a curfew and what kind of pushback might you get from the community?

☐ Risk Assessment: balance the needs of the community to use the road day and night versus the threat of intruders, thieves, and looters.

Genuine Security vs the Illusion of Security

Long ago I came to the realization that in our world there is security and there is the illusion of security.

Genuine security is difficult to achieve as it requires professional attention continuously. Also, real security is NOT convenient or easy and people don't like that. They say they want security but they don't want that security to inconvenience them or change their life in any way.

What you will encounter 99 times out of 100 in the world is the illusion of security. The pathetically amateurish TSA is one of the greatest examples of the illusion of security. They tell you that you cannot take a 16 ounce drink onto the airplane because it could be an explosive. So what do they do with the drink they confiscate from you that could be a bomb? They throw it in a trash can right next to the line of hundreds of people waiting to go through "security".

Closed-circuit TV cameras or surveillance cameras are called "security cameras" by many. Cameras cannot and do not provide security, they just record the incident so you can look at the footage later. No crime was ever halted by a security camera.

Think about it. How many times in a week do you watch a video on your phone of a crime; assault, robbery, stabbing/shooting, etc. All of that footage comes from so-called "security cameras".

Surveillance cameras can only be effective tools for preventing crimes if there is a live human person monitoring them and then reacting to what they see. Passive, unmanned cameras are merely voyeuristic pieces of technology.

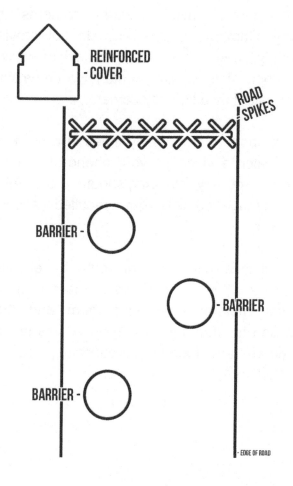

Basic Serpentine Barrier Checkpoint

Patrolling

One tactic that must be practiced *before* the emergency or the crisis is that of patrolling. Patrols can be conducted in vehicles, on foot or on horseback if you have the means. We discussed patrolling in great detail in The Pipe Hitter's Guide to Crushing the Coming Societal Breakdown. If you have not read that book yet, we suggest you do so. Patrolling is in Chapter 3 Team Tactics, of that book.

Additionally, Paul Markel wrote about team tactics and patrolling in his book, Patriot Fire Team: Mission Planner. The entire Patriot Fire Team book series is highly recommended reading for any person wishing to be prepared for civil emergencies.

Chapter 5 Famine, Hunger, Desperation, Psychosis

By Nicholas Orr

During a prolonged civil emergency and/or societal breakdown the threats to your neighborhood and community will INCREASE not decrease as time goes by. During the first few days after the emergency or disaster, opportunistic criminals and degenerates will attack the easy targets first. As soon as it becomes apparent that the police are not coming or that law enforcement is overwhelmed, thugs and looters will hit:

- ☐ Liquor Stores
- ☐ Drug Stores (Walgreen, Rite Aid, etc.)
- ☐ Guns Stores and Pawn Shops
- ☐ Electronics and Appliance Stores
- ☐ Grocery Stores / Big Box Stores, etc.

Along the way, convenience stores and gas stations will be looted and ransacked.

If you own, operate or work at any of the above mentioned places of business, you need to have a plan in place. Do you stay or do you run? If you are an employee whose boss *forbids* you to be armed at work, the choice is not a difficult one to make. If you have your entire life's savings wrapped up in your business, watching it burn to the ground is a hard choice to make. I will not entertain the vile puke of those who say "let it burn, you have insurance". Those kinds of people have never had to make such an insurance claim where the insured always ends up the loser.

Be that as it may, understand that history dictates that the previously highlighted businesses will always be hit first by the criminal element during a riot, emergency, crisis, whatever.

Many of you might be saying, "What about banks?" At the first sign of trouble, bank personnel will put everything of value in the vault and lock it down, ditto for jewelry stores. The average criminal is in no position to break into a bank vault. Besides, who needs cash? Everything is free when you steal it.

The lessons we have from Los Angeles, New Orleans, Minneapolis, Portland, Seattle, Detroit, etc. are that after looting all of the valuables out of the above mentioned places, the criminals will set them on fire. The municipal fire department(s) will very quickly become overwhelmed and these businesses will just burn to the ground. Rioters have historically attacked fire crews as well as law enforcement. Do not expect effective or reliable fire fighting during a riot or civil breakdown.

The **part one** of the civil crisis is actually the most predictable and the easiest for the looters and thugs. Corporate owned stores will be abandoned by the people who work there because it is not "their store", they have no real attachment to the business. The most difficult businesses to take down will be the ones owned by families, the small businesses where the owners have their entire life savings tied up in the store. These are the stores that are most likely to be defended by armed owners; think Rooftop Koreans.

Keep in mind that the criminal element is much like a swarm of locusts. They will destroy all in their path with zero regard for the future. They take and take, they do not plan ahead. These looters will burn down the home supply stores that are filled with vegetable seeds and the means to plant food. They will burn down the grocery stores and destroy the freezers and refrigerators that could be used to store food in the future. If left unchecked, looters and thugs will destroy municipal water treatment facilities, fuel depots, and powerplants. Telephone communication in post-Katrina New Orleans was hampered due to several of the AT&T telecom buildings being damaged or burned down. Does your town, village, municipality have the personnel necessary to protect all of the aforementioned facilities?

The pattern of chaos post-Katrina in New Orleans was for the criminals to take down commercial drugstores first; every RiteAid, CVS, and Walgreen was looted for drugs in the first day or two. After the obvious targets were hit, the thugs moved one to doctors' offices and clinics that had been locked up and abandoned. Next on the list were the 24/7 Urgent Care clinics and then the hospitals that remained open and staffed by emergency workers. The facilities that did not have armed security fell quickly as the staff were held at gunpoint while the thugs cleaned out the pharmacy and the pharmacy carts on each floor.

Keep in mind, not all of the thugs and looters will be random assholes. The drug gangs that operate in every major metropolitan area are organized and led by those who know which drugs are valuable and which are not. These criminals will be given "shopping lists" of the narcotics to be looted from CVS, etc. The constipation and hair growth drugs will be left behind for the lone morons and junkies.

Also, the drug gangs are already armed, they don't need to steal guns before they go to work robbing and looting. When it becomes apparent or obvious that the police are not coming, these gangs will "capture" the drug stores we previously mentioned. Random asshole looters will be sent somewhere else while the Crips, Bloods, Latin Kings, etc. fill their shopping list of narcotics.

At the time of this writing the Mexican Sinaloa Cartel and Cartel Jalisco Nueva Generación (CJNG) are the two more prevalent foreign operations in American cities, but that is subject to chance.

Some of the drug gangs will battle each other for supremacy which is not necessarily a bad thing. In post-Katrina New Orleans there were four different drug gangs battling for control of the area.

I have a friend who worked as armed security at a hospital in New Orleans, post-Katrina. My comrade was attacked by a drug seeking maniac who was using a golf club as a weapon. Having no choice, the security agent was forced to shoot the thug. Such scenes played out all over the metropolitan area.

The thugs and criminal element will spend the first week or two cleaning out obvious and easy targets. Some may venture out into the suburbs or the countryside to pick off easy targets of opportunity. However, they will not be truly desperate, at least not at first.

Before I could complete this book and send it to the printer we witnessed yet another display of animal-like behavior in a big city. Over Christmas weekend, 2022, Buffalo, New York, had a blizzard. Newsflash, Buffalo ALWAYS gets a lot of snow. The response of the criminal element was to loot stores during the snowstorm. These pieces of human filth were not starving, they were opportunistic criminal scum. This is just one more example of the animalistic behavior to which inhabitants of cities will sink in the blink of an eye. Any time the criminal element believes the police are otherwise occupied they will loot and steal.

The second part **(two)** of the civil disorder will take place after the thug element has exhausted the easy targets. Naturally, there are numerous factors at play here that will determine the timeline. How big and how dense is the population? Prior to the civil breakdown, how active were the drug / street gangs? Are the gang leaders known or unknown to law enforcement? Have they been neutralized?

In what condition is the population in general? Are the majority of the people prepared for self-sufficiency or have they been living hand to mouth, check to check? The grocery stores in every major city have approximately 3 days worth of food, before they must be resupplied. Keep in mind that the 3 *days* of food rule only applies if the stores have not been hit by panic buyers or looters. Looters will wipe out a fully-stocked grocery store in a day and leave only wreckage behind.

The weather is also a factor. If the power goes out and it is extremely hot, people will be outside and prowling around. Even under normal conditions, extreme heat waves tend to result in a higher number of calls for local law enforcement. During extreme cold, people will generally shelter from the weather. This can be a positive thing. But, as we witnessed in Buffalo, NY, this cannot be relied upon.

However, cold weather combined with a power outage or lack of reliable energy will find people burning things that should not be burned and trying to heat homes with fire even though they are not designed for that.

Recently, during a cold snap in Texas, numerous people died from accidental fires and carbon-monoxide poisoning. These people had no idea how to deal with such a situation for a few days. Imagine weeks of freezing temperatures and no power.

Consider **part 3**, genuine hunger. When people become hungry, they are both psychologically and physically uncomfortable. Any person who has engaged in deliberate fasting or been in the infantry understands that you are not going to die just because you are hungry and your belly is rumbling.

Nonetheless, consider that the vast majority of the population has NEVER truly been hungry. Yes, there is some genuine poverty in the United States, it is however, rare. The American *poor* are fat. The poor in 3rd world countries are emaciated by hunger. The American poor are malnourished because they eat garbage, but they are not starving by any stretch. Think about it, the American *poor* have mobile phones, internet and flat screen TV's. This situation was deliberately designed by the national government to create a welfare state. The *poor* are dependent upon the welfare state and will support/vote for whomever it is that promises more slop in the trough.

What happens when the government is bankrupt or the food and fuel are not available? What good does a State-issued free food card do you if there is no food in the stores for whatever reason? How will those who are completely dependent upon a welfare state behave when they actually become hungry? Keep in mind, the brains of said people have been malnourished for decades because of the high levels of Omega-6. The impulse control area of their brains does not function properly. How are these people going to react to any kind of hardship or real hunger? Rationally?

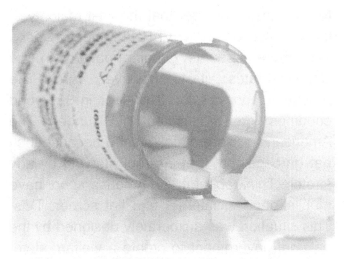

How will people behave when they are cut off from their psychotropic drugs?

Part 4 We have not even considered the epidemic of psychiatric and mood altering prescription drugs. According to one study, 1 in 6 Americans was taking some type of psychiatric drug. A study released in 2022 has the numbers as 1 in 4 Americans. Even if those numbers are high, what if it was only 1 in 10?

Remember, the historical examples we related earlier regarding pharmacies being looted and burned to the ground? How are people who have become addicted to pharmaceutical mood altering or psychiatric drugs going to behave when their supply runs out and they must deal with genuine hardship and discomfort?

In 2020, the people of the United States were shocked (or not) to learn that the majority of the pharmaceutical drugs taken by Americans are not manufactured in the USA, but overseas in China. The plandemic caused supply chain breakdown and shortage/scarcity of some prescription drugs. What will happen to the Rx drug supply chain when there is another global crisis or a war in Asia?

If you want to consider a double-whammy, many of the same people with malnourished brains are also addicted to psychotropic prescription drugs. A global or national crisis can and will interrupt not only the food supply, but the Rx drug supply. What type of behavior can we expect from people in this category?

A rational examination of this situation would conclude that we could expect an increase in suicides, domestic violence, rage and violence directed at strangers, and other anti-social behaviors. The big question would be; is your community prepared to deal with this very realistic problem?

One thing is certain, ignoring the aforementioned realities will not make them go away.

The purpose of this book was not to scare you or to engage in some kind of fear-mongering. We have cited numerous historical examples of civil unrest and the consequences of such. To believe that such unrest, whether localized, national, or worldwide, will never happen again is naive.

Additionally, history has proven that the state or government agencies provide assistance too little too late during true crisis situations. And, as often as not, Federal government agencies create more problems than they solve due to blind bureaucracy, incompetence, and blatant corruption.

If your community has any hope of minimizing damage and destruction during civil unrest and or natural disasters, it will be the people of the community themselves who will make the difference.

We cannot merely wish for the best and hope that all is well. The time to prepare is right now. I believe I speak for all the contributors to this book when I say that our sincere desire is for you to take the lessons laid out herein and become the most resilient, self-sufficient and well-prepared individuals and communities that you can be.

About the Author

Nicolas Orr is the nom de plume for a civilized barbarian, a savage gentleman, with thirty plus years of operational and combat experience in the United States and overseas. The author has carried a gun during innumerable assignments worldwide as a member of the United States Military, as a Military Contractor, and Executive Protection Agent.

Thomas Thrasher is one of the author's favorite characters and the conduit for hardcore, in your face, information delivery and entertainment. The adventures of Thomas Thrasher are chronicled in The Operator Series of books by Nicholas Orr.

Pipe Hitter Books by Nicholas Orr:

A Pipe Hitters Guide to Crushing the Coming Societal Breakdown

A Pipe Hitters Guide to the Citizens Irregular Defense Corps

Other books by Nicholas Orr

The Operator

Sin City: The Operator Book 2

Operation Diomedes: The Operator Book 3

Operation White Feather Part 1, The Operator: Book 4

Operation White Feather Part 2, The Operator Book 5

Field Ops: The Operator Trilogy

Follow Nicholas Orr and get regular updates about his latest projects at,

www.officialnicholasorr.com